M.I.J. Griffin

American Catholic Historical Researches

October 1896

M.I.J. Griffin

American Catholic Historical Researches
October 1896

ISBN/EAN: 9783743463400

Manufactured in Europe, USA, Canada, Australia, Japa

Cover: Foto ©Lupo / pixelio.de

Manufactured and distributed by brebook publishing software
(www.brebook.com)

M.I.J. Griffin

American Catholic Historical Researches

THE

AMERICAN✶CATHOLIC

HISTORICAL RESEARCHES

VOL. XIII.　　　**OCTOBER, 1896.**　　　**NO. 4**

QUARTERLY,　　　*ONE DOLLAR A YEAR.*

DEAR PATRONS:

THE RESEARCHES continues to win the approval of its patrons. Its contributions to Catholic American History are recognized as most valuable. They are devoid of bombast and blunders. They are the original sources of the History of the events they narrate. They are not written to sustain theories or to flatter favorites.

As time passes the value of THE RESEARCHES documents will yearly increase.

The articles contained in the present Number will amply sustain the reputation of the publication and strengthen more the appreciation accorded it.

"OLD MARY JOHNSON."

Another of our village's celebrities, though her fame was principally among the Catholics, was dear "old Mary Johnson." She too was an admirer of "curley-headed Hogan," and adhered to him "a poor persecuted martyr," after his suspension by Bishop Conwell. When he could no longer remain with the other priests in Father Greaton's house, but took up his residence in the small two-story dwelling, as the residence of Mrs. Baker's parents, and which now belonged to St. Mary's Church, Mary Johnson became his housekeeper. I wish I could describe Mary to you as many of our fathers have seen her. She was scarce more than four feet high, lean in proportion, and until old age, active upon her feet; she never walked, she always trotted. If Mr. Swiveler had seen her, he would have declared her a close connection of the Marchioness. I must give you a description of this historical house. It was a two-storied house with attics. From a step on a level with the sidewalk, you entered a box-entry, about four feet by three, which led into Mrs. Baker's "best room." A window on the North side opposite the door of entrance gave you a view of a narrow four foot yard and of the St. Joseph's Residence. To the right of this window was a door leading to the kitchen, or as it was generally called "the living room." As soon as you passed this door, stepping to the right, you might ascend the stairs to the second floor, landing upon a small square entry, between the two rooms and having another flight leading to the attic as it is now styled, then, to the garret. In this entry was a window from which an easy view might be obtained of all who entered the Bishop's house. It was a favorite occupation of "the Gentleman from Limerick" to sit in this entry pretending to read, but in reality watching the incomings and outgoings at the house of his adversary. One afternoon when engaged in this pastime, a committee of three of the trustees of St. Mary's—John Leamy, Richard W. Meade, and John Ashley, waited upon Mr. Hogan, to obtain his signature to a letter they had prepared as from him in reply to the Bishop's Secretary, Rev. Wm. Vincent Harold, O. S. D. Their knock at the door brought Mary from her classic apartment to answer it. It was necessary that she should pass the Reverend gentleman, who, not knowing who was about to visit him, thought he might take a liberty with his little "Dame Durden," he had often taken with the proud damsels of Penn's City.—Noble Mary Johnson! She had clung to Mr. Hogan through

good report and ill, for she thought he was a true priest of God ; she had
heard the current stories, but, to her, these were the inventions of enemies ;
she knew he was censured by his Bishop, but she had been led to believe
the Bishop "an obstinate, ill-informed tyrannical, old dotard." It is true
he had kept very late hours, but Mary was an industrious, cleanly body,
and after a day's hard labor, when she ascended to her garret and had said
her prayers, she recked but little of sublunary affairs. Mr. Hogan did not
attend the sick, so she had no dread of night calls hovering over her inno-
cent slumbers. But, Mr. Hogan, this time, had made a mistake—the blood
of purity suffused her face, the light of insulted virtue flashed from her eye,
and with the strength of an Agnes or a Lucy, she gave the chair a push,
which sent it and its sacrilegious occupant heels over head down the stairs.
Crash went the door, and there lay William and the chair, and "who could
say which was which ?" The gentlemen in waiting hearing the noise,
entered, and what was their amazement to behold their chosen pastor, lying
upon the floor of the kitchen, his well greased locks disheveled, and bruised
more severely than he chose to acknowledge. and the little Heroine of
Willing's Alley standing dishcloth in hand ready to defend herself and
honor. "That woman's crazy," said Mr. H. rising, "without the least
provocation, she threw me down stairs, she's an emissary of Cooper's."
"She's little in size," said John Ashley with a peculiar smile, "but she's
big in strength." From that day poor Mary Johnson was never perfectly
"right in mind." Her self-imposed mission was to drive all dogs out of
Church. Mass or Vespers, or Lenten Service, there was Mary with her
stool, which she placed in the middle of the aisle. Infatuated animal of
the canine species, you made a mistake in entering St. Joseph's Church, if
you thought you would there find a haven of repose for your weary mem-
bers.—Mary Johnson is there ; think not because she is so quiet, telling her
beads, or gazing at the Holy Tabernacle, you can enter unperceived ; you
have not crossed the threshold, no one else may have perceived you, when
up jumps Mary. Now, doggy, doggy, you had better go out—take the
word of a friend and go at once. You need not think to frighten her by
your "bark ;" why, Lion, she's not afraid of your "bite." Rover, none of
your tricks, skip and jump, yes, flourish your interesting *narrative*, you
cannot blarney Mary ; that's as trite as a twice told tale to her. Juno,

poor pet, suppose not that your mistress' skirts shall prove a "Fairy God-mother's cloak" to render you invisible. Doggies, Mary has said that you shall leave the Church, and Mary's *fiat* is irrevocable. Come, nice fellows, come now, come, go out. Is there any rule without an exception? This exterminating statute had one solitary. Every day before first Mass, a tan-colored quadruped walked serenely and stately up the middle aisle, until he arrived at the ten-plate piece of furniture so useful for imparting warmth to man and brute, and there he lay down and slept till service was over, when he rejoined his master at the door. Many wondered why this privi-lege. No reliable data can be found to show when and how or what he did to propitiate the lady of the stool.

For many years, Mary made her home, as a kind of domestic and a kind of protégé, with the family of Mr. Philip Smith. She died a few years since, when an inmate of St. Ann's Widow's Asylum.

It is sad to state that Norah and Mary were not the only persons whose reason was affected by Mr. Hogan's misconduct—happy would it be if the faith of none had been darkened. All who favored him came to an unfor-tunate end. It used to be a common remark. "So and so is dead—wasn't it a fearful death?" "No wonder" would be the response, "they were Hoganites." I know of but two remaining, a very aged lady and her son ; and I must confess I wait with not a little curiosity to hear of their death. The ancient dame I have not seen for years; the son is a penitent of one of Ours, and daily visits the Church and devoutly prays before Him Who has never been petitioned in vain for pardon ; and if humble prayer can avert the temporal punishment due to certain sins, I hope this death will be a proof of it. It is also sad to notice that the son of one of the leaders of that unholy schism—whose memory his Country will cherish for ages, if she lasts so long, as her savior—died yesterday, Nov. 6th, 1872, outside of the pale of the Church, and his funeral services are to take place at St. Mark's Protestant Episcopal Church—Truly the sins of the fathers are visited upon the children to many generations.

[This was Gen. George G. Meade. ED. RESEARCHES.]

[WOODSTOCK LETTERS, Vol. III, No. 1. JAN. 1874.]

BISHOP CONWELL OF PHILADELPHIA AND REV. WM. HOGAN

THE SCHISMATIC. THE "CAPTURE" OF ST. MARY'S--THE

ELECTION RIOT OF 1822.

Upon the arrival Very Rev. Ludovicus Barth in July, 1820, the general expectation of clerks and laity was that Mr. Hogan would be dismissed from St. Joseph's, but in this they were sadly mistaken. The very day of his arrival visiting the School house, one very dear to me related to him the reports concerning "the new priest," for the truth of some of which she could vouch, having seen them. "Susan," said the Very Reverend Administrator, "he's Irish and the new Bishop is Irish, let the Irish settle it among themselves." On returning to Conewago, towards the end of the month he appointed Mr. Hogan, an unknown young man, with no papers to show that he had ever been ordained, to preside at the meeting of the trustees of St. Mary's over the Rev. Patrick Kenny and Terence McGirr, who had for years officiated at St. Joseph's. They, together with Rev. Michael Hurley O. S. A., immediately sent a protest to Most Rev. Ambrose Maréchal, D. D., Archbishop of Baltimore. This act of Very Rev. Ludovicus Barth was the proximate beginning of the troubles that distracted the Church of Philadelphia for over twelve years.

At the latter part of August, and again towards the close of September, Rev. Ludovicus Barth was at St. Joseph's, and again and again the misconduct of Mr. Hogan was reported to him, and his invariable answer was "the new Bishop will soon be here." Rev. Fathers McGirr and Kenny having to live in the same house with the person, could say but little, but Father Hurley, who made the "Limerick boy," the staple each Sunday's discourse, remarking upon this answer of the Very Rev. Administrator said: "St. Michael may be here to-morrow and St. Michael may be here the next day, but Lucifer is here to-day."

At the beginning of December, 1820, Right Rev. Henry Conwell, D. D., second Bishop of Philadelphia, arrived at St. Joseph's, and immediately began his pastoral duties. His first record reads:

"die 5 10bris   } Cornelius Steel, filius Jac. et Elizae. natus
a. R. R. H. Conwell, } Philadae. Septembris die 29. Susceptus fuit a
Epo. Phae.   } Sara Bowles Sola.

Poor Bishop Conwell ! his was an eventful life. When he was appointed Vicar-General of the Archdiocese of Armagh, he thought his ambition satisfied, but when offered the Bishopric of Philadelphia, though at an age when most men are thinking to retire and prepare for death, he was ready to say : "Lo, here I am ; send me." One of his first acts, upon receiving the announcement of his appointment, was to write to his eldest niece to accompany him to America, saying that she had been servant long enough to her brothers and sisters, now she should be mistress in the palace of her uncle, the Lord Bishop. One of Bishop Conwell's greatest mistakes was the surrounding himself with so many nieces and nephews.

Bishop Conwell was a man of no mean ability ; his latinity was classical, and especially his ecclesiastical Latin was much admired. He was a Greek scholar, spoke French fluently and Spanish and Italian with but little difficulty. His knowledge of theology, moral and dogmatic, was solid, and he had not neglected the study of Canon Law. Unfortunately he was not a fluent preacher in his native language ;—but it must not be supposed that he was an ungrammatical or inelegant speaker. Those pamphlets that were so numerous some years ago, purporting to be reports of his sermons at St. Mary's, were the productions of his enemies,—of John T. Sullivan and John Ashley, or it was supposed so at the time. The Bishop's personal appearance was not unpleasing. When he arrived he was over seventy, tall, straight, muscular, and, when occasion required, not deficient in dignity. Though of uncertain temper, he was kind-hearted, forgiving, and a bountiful giver. Had he possessed the eloquence, or even the polished manner of Wm. Vincent Harold, the misstep of Very Rev. Ludovicus Barth would not have been so prolific in evil.

Upon his arrival, he found domiciled in his own family a young man, of whose misconduct he had heard reports in Ireland ; and a few days after his arrival he received a letter from Bishop Connelly of New York, stating in full his disobedience to him. When questioned as to his exeat, his answer was the same given some months before to Father Kenny, that his papers would soon arrive. Being a stranger in the country and not wishing to disapprove of the acts of the Very Rev. Father Administrator, Bishop Conwell wrote for advice to his superior, Most Rev. Ambrose Maréchhal'

D. D., and on the 20th of December, publicly withdrew from Wm. Hogan, all faculties he might seem to have derived from the *quasi* approval of Very Rev. Ludovicus Barth. This was the signal for revolt, and a sad, sad revolt it proved.

The beginning of 1821 finds Bishop Conwell officiating at St. Mary's, without any trouble from Mr. Hogan or the trustees; his Assistant being Rev. George Sheufelter, and Rev. James Cummiskey, whom the Bishop afterwards surnamed the "Reverend Pedler," from the fact of his employing agents, and himself travelling at times, to sell Catholic books, especially "Christian Perfection" by Fr. Rodriguez, S. J. He was an elder brother of Eugene Cummiskey, for many years the Catholic bookseller of Philadelphia,

Another very embarassing circumstance in the early history of the Church in this Diocese was the visit of the Right Reverend John England, D. D., first Bishop of Charleston, to the City of Philadelphia. Before this time, the trustees knew they were insubordinate, but when they gathered from the Bishop that they were on an equality with their diocesan and ought to, not *might* or *could* appeal to Rome, offering himself, to be appointed their agent, their conduct became insupportable. The Bishop, i. e. the Bishop of Philadelphia, remained at home at St. Joseph's, which Church he now made his Cathedral, and the faithful Catholics flocked around him. Shortly after he enlarged the Church to almost its present dimensions, that it might accommodate the crowds. In June he added to the number of his assistants, Rev. Samuel Cooper, of happy memory, and in the latter part of the month ordained Rev. Thomas Heyden.

The year 1822, in Philadelphia, is ever memorable with an unhappy remembrance. The early part of the year was employed by the trustees in building new pews and renting them to their partisans to influence the vote at the coming elections. The trustees took possession of the Church and lest any bishopite should,—a great maxim at the time, was "possession is nine tenths of the law"—it was kept barricaded with a watchman constantly on guard. My father with other hot-headed young Irishmen determined that get possession of the Church before the day of election, they *would*, if they had to sacrifice a limb, yea, life for it. Good Father Cooper was taken into confidence but he disapproved of the plot. "No matter," said they, "that was because he was not an Irishman and only half a Catholic." Such of our family as were living at that time resided in Marshall's Court, now called Landis Street. The windows of the house overlooking St. Mary's graveyard, it was a very favorable spot for observing the enemy's manœuvres, but there was difficulty in the way, my mother, like Father Cooper, was not an Irishman and only half a Catholic. The house where, I think, Bishop Wood was born, but however that may be, the house where Bishop Kenrick afterwards took up his residence and began his Seminary, was chosen as a "*point d'appui*," whilst the tombstones made many a convenient *cachette* for watching the movements of the besieged. Many a mysterious bundle was seen carried by strong men into the house of the God of peace, the Church built with Father Greaton's money, but try as they would the watchman could never be caught napping. I hope our good bishopites never suffered from rheumatism from the many hours they spent on the damp ground of early Spring, behind the eulogistic monuments of the dead. The Monday of Holy Week came, time was growing short. It was well nigh noon, the daughter of the vigilant watchman is seen approaching, forty of the forty-six days of abstinence are passed, —what's that which smells so savory? never mind John M———, hidden behind the tomb of Bishop Egan, you have tasted nothing for eighteen hours save water and a drop, just a little drop, of American wine, what does it concern you what a Roganite has for dinner? Hark! was that a whistle? no it cannot be, it sounded but an echo. What's the matter? From the *point d'appui* creeps like a serpent a man of forty—from a second-story window leaps like a hare a stalwart youth of twenty. What! are they going to burst as burglars into the holy Church! No they intend to enter through the principal exit, if not entrance. For once the hungry watchman has been caught off his guard. The nicely-browned catties with fragrant mocha, and hot biscuts were too much for hungry Barney B———, he forgot to bolt and bar the door. The citadel is taken and Barney B———, almost before he had done away with one luscious catty, is a prisoner, elbow bound to elbow. The schoolmaster writes a hasty note to my Lord, the Bishop, announcing the capture. The "female daughter" of the captive was deputed to carry the important document to Willing's Alley. In the meanwhile the victors scoured the field of victory; the galleries were found lined with bricks and stones, and when Father McGirr came, the unwilling bearer of a brief but explicit despatch from the Commander-in-General, he found more than one pistol in the holy tabernacle. The despatch read thus: "Go home and mind your own business. † Henry Conwell, Epius. Philaae." Just think of this hapless triumvirate, for nearly a month they and others had risked so many dangers to obtain for their Bishop his own Church, and now when success was theirs, their thanks were, "Go home and mind your own business." Father McGirr released Barney B———, and John, Pat and———with spoiled appetites, hastened home to their catfish, coffee and biscuits.

On Tuesday of Easter week, the annual election of trustees of St. Mary's Church took place. The Bishopites might as well have let it pass unnoticed, it was already determined that the Leamy, Meade party should be the elected. But no, if they did not get the election they should, at least, have the fight. Sunrise saw young men and buxom maids, who had no vote, trudging in from Germantown, Manayunk, and Chester, and Darby, and even from over the waters, to do and die, for Bishop and for Church. It was this day of days, that an aged gentleman uttered the memorable threat: "if they do not treat the Bishop better I'll go over till Jarsey and niver come back till Americay agin." But this is no joking matter, it was no comedy, it was in more respects than one a tragedy. Persons at this day can tell you, how bricks were thrown from the windows of the Church upon the head of the hapless Bishopites whilst striving to vote,* how young men would stand in Indian file and the backmost would ascend a cellar door, so as to give greater impetus, whilst the head of the foremost made a most convenient battering ram to butt between the kidneys of some thoughtless Hoganite, who was laughing at the funny sight of

* Henry Smith M. D., son-in-law of Dr. Horner who sometime afterwards became a Catholic. The house of Dr. Smith's father, was directly opposite to St. Mary's. The Doctor was at that time a lad of fifteen, but his description of events is very graphic.

some Bishopite rendered *hors de combat* and hastening home with bloody head or crippled limb. Both parties can tell you how the iron rail swayed backwards and forwards, like a reed shaken by the wind, and at last fell with a crash, that caused a piercing shriek of anguish from many a wife and mother, kneeling in the corner of her room, with her little ones, praying for the dear ones. "O God, save the father of my children," was the cry of one most dear to me, as she heard the crash. "Susan," was the stoical remark of her Quaker ancestress "thou seest now what these Catholics are." That carping Quakeress, some years after, became a Catholic, and her bones repose beneath the altar of St. Mary's Church, Lebanon. Yes ! that iron railing fell with a crash, and many a heart that beat loyally for Catholicity, for a time, was stilled in anguish, and the casket of many a whole-souled Catholic was mangled and disfigured for life. And some of those, who then left the Church of their Baptism, might tell you how while Rt. Rev. Henry Conwell, D. D., and Rev. Samuel Cooper, and Rev. Terence McGirr, and Rev. Patrick Kenny, yea, and Rev. Wm. Vincent Harold, O. S. D., stood at the N. E. Corner of 4th street and Willing's Alley, *oil-stock* in hand and *pixis* near the trembling heart, to follow the bleeding forms of the wounded into the house of Charles Johnson, Sr., and other good Samaritans. Mr. Wm. Hogan, in concert with the delicate, lady-like daughters of rebel Catholics raised shouts of laughter that could be heard above the shrieks of the wounded ;—which unnatural cachinnations, thanks be to a God, who can draw good out of evil I has brought more than one Protestant who heard it, into the happy fold of Christ's Church. It was truly a fearful day, still with all the odds against them, Joseph Synder, John Carrell, Sr., Cornelius Tiers, Dennis McCready, Nicholas Stafford, William Myers, Nicholas Ealing, and James Eneu, Sr., were elected trustees of St. Mary's Church receiving 437 votes, although J. Cadwalader, Esq., decided that John Leamy, John Ashley and their party received 497. It may be true that they did, but the excess came from the votes of the occupants of those pews which had been erected after the withdrawal of the Bishop whose consent was necessary, as President according to the charter. Unhappy day! The difficulty still remained.

Shortly before this fracas, Rev. Wm. Vincent Harold, had returned to Philadelphia, at the request of Bishop Conwell. Between the time of the invitation and his arrival, slanderous tongues had been at work, and the sleeping jealousy of "my Lord" had been awakened, so that when Father Harold arrived he was coldly received, which to him was a new style of reception, and which his natural pride never forgot, but, I hope, forgave. In the meanwhile the interposition of the civil authorities had been invoked, and Mayor Waterman standing upon the tomb of Bishop Egan proclaimed Right Reverend Henry Conwell, Second Roman Catholic Bishop of Philadelphia, the legal pastor of St. Mary's Church.

For a short while there was peace, and Rev. Wm. Vincent Harold acted as pastor, but the truce was of short duration and the sacrilegious Hogan again officiated at the altar of St. Mary's.

[WOODSTOCK LETTERS, Vol. III, No. 1, JAN. 1874.]

[On June 29th, 1896, Mr. Francis Harold Duffee, of Philadelphia, died. He was an altar-boy at St. Mary's at time of "the Hogan trouble." His "REMINISCENCES OF REV. WM. HOGAN AND REV. WM. V. HAROLD" appeared in THE RESEARCHES, April 1891. Mr. Duffee abandoned the Faith of his youth. A few weeks before his death he told me he often went to St. Mary's Church and remained there "for hours" in recollections of his early years. ED. RESEARCHES.]

LETTERS OF BISHOP CARROLL TO ARCHBISHOP TROY

OF DUBLIN.

The following important letters of Rev John Carroll, our First Prelate, to Archbishop Troy, of Dublin, are from copies made for Mr. F. X. Reuss, of Philadelphia, who permits THE RESEARCHES to present them to the public.

BALTIMORE, AUG. 11TH, 1788·

MY LORD,

I was honored with your Grace' letter of May 16th, by Rev'd. Mr. Ryan, who arrived at Philadelphia the first of this month, and is now with me, I am happy in taking the occasion to open a correspondence with a prelate of your distinguished character, and hope your Grace will allow me to apply to you with confidence and liberty in all matters which may intervene between this Country and Ireland, relative to the welfare of Religion, Mr. Ryan I will endeavor to place, agreeably to himself, and advantageously to some Catholics destitute of all spiritual assistance. He is not willing to accept an appointment in the country, in one of the Western Counties of Pennsylvania, where a large colony of Irish Catholics are soliciting a priest and offer him a maintainance. He has turned his eyes upon Charleston, South Carolina, where a clergyman is likewise wanted' my very good friend Mr. O'Brien of New York has informed your Grace, of the reason I have to be dissatisfied with the unaccountable conduct of the Rev. Mr. S—— —, lately returned to Ireland, I should remain perfectly easy in the self-conviction of having afforded him no cause of dissatisfaction, but quite the contrary, were it not that misrepresentation may deprive this country of the services of some valuable assistance from Ireland. To prevent this, I have written fully to a gentleman of your city, Mr. Mulcaile, whom Mr. O'Brien recommended to me, and with whose character he brought me acquainted, I shall desire him to communicate the

contents to your Lordship that you may be convinced with how little can-
dour Mr. S——— has conducted himself in this business, and that no
impressions may be received as if I were not disposed to give employment
to as many virtuous and well informed clergymen, as a maintainance can
be procured for. But one thing must be fully impressed upon their minds,
that no pecuniary prospects or worldly comforts must enter into the
motives for their crossing the Atlantic to this Country. They will find
themselves much disappointed, labour, hardships, of every kind, coarse
living, and particularly great scarcity of wine, (espescially out of the towns)
must borne with, sobriety in drink is expected from clergymen to a great
degree. That which in many parts of Europe would be esteemed no more
than a cheerful and allowable enjoyment of a friendly company, would be
regarded here in our clergy as an unbecoming excess. Your Lordship will
excuse this detail, and know how to ascribe it to its proper motive, that
gentlemen applying to come to this country, may know what I expect.

I have the honor to be, with greatest veneration and respect.

MY LORD,

YOUR GRACE' MOST OBEDIENT AND

HUMBLE SERVANT,

J. CARROLL.

Notes by F. X. Reuss.

Letter No. 1. The Rev. Mr. S———.

This was, no doubt, Rev. Patrick Smyth who assailed Bp. Carroll,
because of Father Graessel being appointed to Phila. (See Letter 2nd).
For Biog'l. sketch of Smyth, see *Cogan's* "History of the Diocese of
Meath."

The Rev. Mr. O'Brien, was Rev. William O'Brien, O. P. who was in
Phila. at about 1785–6.

DUMFRIES, VIRGINIA.

JULY 2ND. 1789.

MY LORD,

A few days before I left Baltimore with a view of visiting a few of our scattered congregations, I was honored with your Grace' letter of February, in which you have in a manner the most obliging, communicated to me the intelligence of Mr. S———'s pamphlet, shall I call it——— or libel, I had received, a week or two before—the pamphlet itself from a printer in Philadelphia. I reserved to myself to write to your Grace, with the thankfulness which is due to you, and fully, as soon as I should return to Baltimore. But having this moment met, accidentally, a gentleman of character, who sails in two days for Cork, I would not resist the opportunity of informing your Grace, that I will draw up a few observations on the pamphlet as soon as I can get a little leisure, and send them for your reading and that of those other Rev. Prelates who have in a manner so obliging, prevented the intended bad effects of the malicious publication, you will add to other obligations that of presenting my respectful thanks to those Fathers of our Church, and will excuse this uncouth piece of paper, the best I could get in a little tavern where I found the bearer of this.

I have the honour to be, with greatest respect.

MY LORD,

YOUR GRACE' MOST OBLIGED AND HUMBLE SERVANT.

J. CARROLL.

MOST REV. DR. JOHN TROY.

DUBLIN.

[A copy of this pamphlet—the only one known in this country—is in the Catholic Archives of America at Notre Dame University.

"The printer in Philadelphia" who sent copy to Carroll was—no doubt—Mathew Carey. ED. RESEARCHES.]

BALTIMORE, NOV. 9TH, 1789.

MY LORD,

I did myself the honor of writing a few lines to your Lordship from Virginia, the last of June, or the beginning of July. I then returned my sincere thanks for your great and generous endeavor to discountenance a pamphlet full of falsehood and malignity, and I requested your Grace, to be the interpreter of my sentiments of gratitude of the Most Rev. Prelates, who joined your Lordship so readily in condemning it. I lament with your Lordship that there are not more clergymen in the United States, they are large enough, and offer a field wide enough for many more labourers. But unfortunately almost all who offer their services have great expectations of livings, high salaries &c; and these our country does not afford, most of the stations to which salaries are annexed, are occupied; and I find few, or, to speak more properly, I find none willing to commit themselves entirely to the care of Providence, and to seek to gather congregations, and livings, of consequence, by fixing themselves in places where no missioners have preceeded them. Your Grace knows, it was thus religion was propagated in every age of the Church. If clergymen animated with this spirit will offer their services, I will receive them with the greatest cheerfulness, and direct their zeal where there is greatest prospect of success; and well make no manner of distinction between seculars and regulars.

I AM WITH GREATEST VENERATION AND RESPECT,

MY LORD,

YOUR LORDSHIP'S MOST OBT. AND HUMBLE SERVANT,

J. CARROLL.

LONDON, JULY 23D.
No. 28, King Street, Bloomsbury.

MY LORD,

I was favored with your Grace's most obliging letters of January 25th, about two months ago, and would have sooner acknowledged the honor done to me, had I not been in daily expectation of setting out for Europe, which, however was not in my power before June 9th. I am now on my voyage to England for consecration. When the subject of an American Bishopric was first started, I received so pressing an invitation from a most respectable Catholic gentleman in England, that I unawarily promised to be consecrated in his Chapel if the appointment should fall to my lot. Had it been otherwise, I should have hesitated between Ireland, the land of my forefathers, and Canada, though, on the whole I flatter myself that my going to England may be attended with some advantages to the cause of Religion within my extensive diocese, It is probable that I will hear much on the subject of the Oath when I am in England, hitherto I have never seen it, though I have heard of the disagreement among the VV. AA.* I shall be very cautious in forming, and more so in uttering, any opinions while I am there. I shall pay every attention to the subject mentioned in your Grace's seperate letter, I am happy to inform you that Messrs Flemming, whom I have placed in Philadelphia and Burke,* who supplies Mr. O'Brien's absence in New York, give general satisfaction. The former writes all those talents which conciliate esteem and love, and serve for the most useful purposes, the latter is moral, assiduous, and disinterested. Another of your brethern in Religion, Mr. Keating, from Lisbon, was just arrived when I left Baltimore. He is much commended by Mr. Flemming, and will be fixed near Philadelphia.

Mr. O'Brien has been to the Havanna, is gone to La Vera Cruz, and in his last letter from the former place, informs me of his intention to cross the Isthmus of Panama, go to Acapulco, Lima, &c., and return to New York in 1793, when he hopes to have collected sufficient to pay off their debts in New York, and finish their church.

  I HAVE THE HONOR TO BE WITH GREATEST VENERATION.
   MY LORD,
    YOUR GRACE'S MOST OBEDIENT SERVANT,
      J. CARROLL.

* VV. AA. Vicars Apostolic.
* BURKE. Rev. Michael Burke, O. P.

MY LORD,

What excuse shall I offer to your Lordship for my long delay in acknowledging the honour of your most obliging favour of August 5th ? I received, with all the pleasure which the subject would admit, your Lordship's congratulations on the event which has lately taken place, and which is a matter of great consequence, and, I may add, of some consequence to the cause of Religion. I believe that I told your Lordship before the reasons which determined my choice on England for consecration. I flatter myself that my voyage hither has not been unprofitable to the cause over which it is now our common duty to watch in preference to everything else.

Mr. Donnellan has, within these few days, communicated to me the papers you mention. I have read them attentively, and they are such as I humbly conceive would be of benefit if more generally communicated. Since my arrival I have carefully avoided taking any part in the present controversy amongst the Catholics, though I have been urged on all sides. If I had seen any prospect of bringing the principles on each side of the question to a good understanding with each other, most certainly I would have attended much more than I have done to the cause in controversy, and probably should have formed a very decided opinion. At present I can only say, that the oath, in its present form, appears to me inadmissable; that it implies a renunciation of the pastoral powers of the successor of St. Peter ; and that its obvious meaning is different from that which the advocates for the oath affix to it. This I have not said to a soul excepting now to your Lordship, and even to you I deliver this opinion, not as one which is founded on much investigation, but as one which forced itself on my mind when I read the oath. My baggage has been on board some days: the wind keeps the ship in the river, which I hope to leave very shortly. I was greatly obliged to their Lordships (of your province) who offered me their congratulations through your Lordship. May God pour his blessings plentifully on your and their arduous labours for the extension of the faith !

I shall always esteem it a happiness and honour to hear from you. Cardinal Antonelli, in a late letter, recommended me to let your recommendation accompany all priests who go from Ireland to America. In consequence I referred to your Lordship for such recommendation, a Mr. Phelan, a Capuchin friar and postulant for our Mission.

I have the honour to be, with the utmost respect,

MY LORD,

YOUR LORDSHIP'S MOST OBEDIENT SERVANT,

J. CARROLL.

LONDON, OCTOBER 3D, 1790.

BALTIMORE, AUGUST 24, 1791.

MY LORD,

I recur to your Lordship with the utmost confidence in every concern of religion, where your advice, direction, or co-operation can be obtained. Such is my esteem for your Grace, and the abilities to direct and guide with which God has blessed you, not only for the good of your own Country, but also, I trust, of this. I stand now in need of three clergymen for the service of poor abandoned Catholics. They promise faithfully to provide a comfortable support for their pastors. As I know no country but Ireland which can supply our wants, I presume to make them known to your Grace, not doubting but you will, with your wonted zeal, make known my desire to some virtuous clergymen. Allow me to request, that none may be selected for this service, of whose fitness your Grace has not the fullest conviction, either from personal knowledge or from such testimony as is entirely satisfactory. The stations for which they are destined require men of solid and approved virtue, for they will be left in great measure out of the reach of control or eye of inspection ; consequently, unless they be thoroughly established in the habits of a sacerdotal purity of manners, sobriety, and of zeal, they will not be qualified for that destination which is intended. Besides this first requisite of an irreproachable conduct, strength of bodily health is absolutely necessary to undergo the fatigues and constant hardships of labour and diet to which they will

be exposed. Finally, they will be placed amongst strangers and bitter
enemies to our faith and Church, who will often seek opportunities of
engaging in controversy, and not unfrequently with much dexterity. This
renders it advisable and indispensable for the clergymen to be gentlemen
fond of study, of improved understandings, and, above all, skilled in
theological science. If your Lordship can find out such, disengaged from
more important employment, and zealous to bestow their labours in my
diocese, I shall ever esteem it a great favour to receive them from your
hands. If your Grace can obtain a character corresponding to that which
I have drawn, of the Rev. Mr. Henry Cambell, curate of Belfast, I shall
wish him to be one of the three. I received lately a letter from him, well
and sensibly written. He says, that Dr. Karney, President of the Seminary
at Paris, the Bishop of Down, in whose diocese he now is, and the Archbishop of Armagh, his native bishop, will bear testimony to his conduct.
I shall refer him to your Grace, and if approved of by you, I will receive him.

Our friend Mr. O'Brien was well in Mexico last May, collecting dollars
for his church in New York. His vicar *Mr. Michael Burke*, of your order,
the exellent Mr. Flemming, and his young friend Mr. Keating, are likewise well.

I have the honor to be, with the greatest respect and veneration.

MY LORD,

YOUR GRACE'S MOST OBEDIENT AND HUMBLE SERVANT,

† J., BISHOP OF BALTIMORE.

BALTIMORE, APRIL 16TH, 1792.

MY LORD,

I am duly honoured with your Grace's favours of Jan. 2nd and Feb. 4th,
and highly obliged to you, as I have had cause often to be, for your
Lordship's continued attention to the advantage and progress of true
religion and sound morality in my diocese, which are so much dependant,
under God, on the good conduct of the clergymen employed in it. I paid
due attention to your account of Mr. Campbell, who, in a late letter,
declines for the present his proposed voyage to America, and from which I

collected that he was deeply immerged in the politics of the North of Ireland. If Mr. Paine be the master of his opinions on government, as, from some expressions I presume he is, he has fallen into bad hands indeed, for if Paine's principles be true, government is far from being a blessing. I mean hereby government, its form and constitutions, which will never be fixed or steady, but continually liable to be dissolved by the turbulence and and endless variety of human systems.

I understood by Mr. Campbell's letter, that a principal mover in the business of the North, and in coaliting Catholics and Presbyterians, is a person from this Country of the name of Digges. With him I am not acquainted, but pretty well with his character, and I am induced, by a solicitous regard for the Catholics of Ireland, and for your Lordship in particular to mention some circumstances relating to Mr. Digges, which need not be mentioned further than you will find it necessary. He is of respectable family and connections in this country, no one more so; in his early youth he was guilty of misdemeanours here, indicating rooted depravity, but amazing address, but even this could not screen him, and his friends, to rescue him from the hands of justice, and themselves from dishonour, sent him out of the country. He went first to Lisbon, where fresh misconduct compelled him to seek refuge elsewhere. He arrived in England at the beginning of the American War, and with his wonted address and insinuating manners, engaged himself deeply in the familiarity of all the Americans in England, and the lords and commons who combated the ministry on the subject of the American War. He even wrote such good accounts of the designs of England to the American negotiators at Paris, that they conceived the highest confidence in his zeal for their cause, and entrusted him with the disposal of large sums of money for the relief of American prisoners languishing in England; but all this time, as it was afterwards known, he was a spy for Lord North, and employed by him in some important business. He never applied the money sent him. After the war he continued his malpractices, but has sufficient dexterity, by shifting his scenes of action, and displaying extraordinary abilities, to gain confidence for a time. You may easily conceive how dangerous it would be for such a man to obtain any degree of trust in the management of your concerns, which require such heads and hearts.

Your acquaintance the Rev. Mr. O'Brien, will return from Mexico, having had considerable success, but not equal to his expectation.

My sincere and fervent prayer is, that it may please Almighty God to preserve harmony amongst the Roman Catholics of Ireland, and dispose them to listen to the lessons of wisdom, which you will give them, and grant them that degree of liberty, and of the civil rights of their country, which will make them happy here and hereafter.

I AM, WITH THE UTMOST ESTEEM AND VENERATION

MY VERY GOOD LORD,

YOUR GRACE'S MOST OBEDIENT AND HUMBLE SERVANT,

† J., BISHOP OF BALTIMORE.

BALTIMORE, AUGUST 11, 1792.

MY LORD,

Your Lordship's last letters gave me little encouagement to hope for any clerical coadjutors from your Kingdom. Even the Rev. Mr. Gilmer has not yet arrived, although I had the honour of writing to your Lordship immediately after the receipt of your letter, and requesting his immediate departure, engaging to pay here at his arrival ten guineas, if he came immediately. This money is deposited with me by a body distressed Catholics, who are without a clergymen, and who wait impatiently for his arrival.

Notwithstanding the discouragement given in your last letter, I still make bold to request your Lordship to make known, as occasion may offer, the very great distress under which this diocese labours for want of clergymen, and the repeated assurances which I receive from those who are in want of them, that they shall be comfortably provided. If your respectable brethern in the episcopacy will be so condescending as to communicate this notice, and be very careful not to give dimissorials to, or recommend any, whose character and principles are not immaculate, I would receive with the utmost joy six such clergymen.

I have been informed lately that your divisions are likely to be healed and that under the authority of your name, and attention to your prudent and vigorous advice, the Catholics of Ireland are likely to obtain a re-establishment of other and more important civil rights than have yet been conferred on them. God grant that this may be true.

Our religious establishments are multiplying in these States. But owing to the fewness of our clergy, divine service is kept in them so irregularly, that they do not produce half the good effects which otherwise they would. Praying that it may be in your Grace's power, as much as it is your inclination, to remove the obstacles I have mentioned, I assure you with veneration and the utmost esteem and respect, that I have the honour to be.

> MY LORD,
>> YOUR GRACE'S MOST OBEDIENT SERVANT.
>>> † J., BISHOP OF BALTIMORE.

> BALTIMORE, MAY 10, 1798.

MY DEAR AND VERY HONOURED LORD.

The Rev. Mr. Gallagher presented me with your Lordship's favour of Feb. 3rd. As his talents are commended by so good a judge as your Grace, and he gave indeed a very pleasing specimen of them in a sermon before the congregation of this town, I have appointed him to the care of Charlestown, South Carolina, which is a place requiring a man of considerable abilities, which Mr. Gallagher possesses, and great purity of manners, which I hope is another trait of his character.

We are waiting with great anxiety, not only for the news to be expected on French affairs, but those likewise which concern so deeply the fate of Catholicity in Ireland.

I have the honour to remain, with the greatest esteem and veneration.

> MY LORD,
>> YOUR LORDSHIP'S MOST OBEDIENT AND OBLIGED SERVANT,
>>> † J., BISHOP OF BALTIMORE.

ST. MARY'S, (PHILADELPHIA,) PASTORAL RESIDENCE.

Without going into the legal records of the ground and prior owners, it will suffice to say that a Doctor Gorman occupied the house prior to its purchase by Rev. Jeremiah Keiley, pastor of St. Mary's in 1830. As early as Sept. 1831, it was opened as the "Catholic Seminary," of which Father Keiley was *Supervisor* and a Mr. Nugent, Prefect and Principal Teacher of the Schools.

The course of education embraced of Greek, Latin, French, Spanish, Italian, English, Elocution, Writing, Arithmetic, Geography, History, use of the Globes, Book keeping, Algebra, Geometry and, if required, the highest branches of Mathematics with Moral and Natural Philosophy. The other branches were taught by gentlemen of high attainments and long experience.

Who knows the names of any of them ?

Examinations were held semi annually and gentlemen of literary reputation examined the pupils. Each branch was taught in a separate room by a master who had not over 25 pupils.

The terms were $12.50 a quarter for the Classical Department and $6 for the English Department. A charge of 50 cts. was made for pens and ink and $1 for fuel in winter.

This Seminary must have had such a success as to induce Father Keiley to hope that he might establish a larger institution near the city. He accordingly sold in 1834 the house, which was his personal property, to the Trustees of St Mary's and on Nov. 9th, 1834, delivered his farewell sermon to the congregation. On January 1st, 1835, he opened a Catholic Seminary at what is now North Laurel Hill Cemetery. Do my readers know that this grand city of the dead where the great and wealthy of our citizens are buried was once a Catholic school ground ?

Prof. Nicholas Maguire once Principal of the Philadelphia High School, and now Principal of the Horace Binney Public School, Spruce below Sixth, was in 1835, a teacher in Father Keiley's Laurel Hill Seminary.

The institution did not succeed and was closed in December 1835.

The house next to St. Mary's Church—then No. 118—cost the Trustees $4,700, subject to $210 annual ground rent.

After its purchase in 1834, in the latter part of the year the clergy of St. Mary's moved into it. They had been living two doors below.

The present pastoral residence was built in 1886 on the site of the old structure.

MARTIN I. J. GRIFFIN.

LETTER OF WASHINGTON TO COL. JOHN FITZGERALD HIS

CATHOLIC AID DE CAMP.

WASHINGTON, Nov. 5, 1895.—At a meeting of the Columbia Historical Society in this city last night the following interesting and hitherto unpublished letter of Washington's was read and elicited much discussion :

VALLEY FORGE, FEB. 28, 1778.

DEAR SIR :

This instant returning from the Committee, and finding the post here, you must put up with a line or two in acknowledgement of your favor of the 16th last., from York, instead of a long letter, which it was my inten-tion to have written you.

I thank you sincerely for the part you acted at York respecting C——y after—— and believe with you that matters have and will turn out different to what that party expected. G——s has involved himself in his letters to me in the most absurd contradictions, M——has brought himself into a scrape, that he does not know how to get out of, with a gentlemen of this State, and C——, as you know, is sent upon an expedition which all the world knew, and the event has proved was not practicable. In a word, I have good deal of reason to believe that the machination of this junta will recoil upon their own heads, and be a means of bringing some matters to light, which by getting me out of the way, some of them thought to conceal.

Remember me in the most affectionate terms to all my old friends and acquaintences in Alexandria, and be assured that with unfeigned regard, I am dear sir, your affectionate friend,

GO. WASHINGTON.

[The blanks in the above letter are to be filled as follows: G——s, Gates ; C——y, Conway ; M——, Mifflin.]

This valuable contribution to history was exhibited by Dr. James Dudley Morgan, to whose great-uncle by marriage, Col. John Fitzgerald, of Alexandria, a member of Washington's staff, the letter was addressed.

Dr. Morgan explained that Washington undoubtedly referred in his letter to the schemes of Generals Gates, Conway and Mifflin, a trio of Revolutionary heroes whom Washington suspected to have formed a cabal to depose him from the commmand of the army.

Everybody present enjoyed the sensation that Washington's letter created. Librarian Spofford simply gloated over it, and among the others who read and re-read the age stained manuscript were the venerable Rev. Dr. Sunderland, Rev. T. DeWitt Talmage, Hon. John Kasson, and Dr. J. M. Toner, President of the society.

The one to whom the letter, was written was a Catholic. The possessor of it and the President o: the Society at which it was made public are Catholics.

ST. JOSEPH'S IN 1808.

BILLS OF EXPENSES, FOR REPAIRS TO THE CHURCH.

In May, 1883, amongst a lot of old papers deemed useless, I found a package marked "Statement of the expenses of repairs in Willing Alley" £510 11s 6d. It proved to be the bills for the work of repairing the house in Willing's Alley. This was in 1808. It may be interesting now to give the items:

Laborers' bill for pulling down wall and digging yard, cistern, etc. (Wm. Habrick), $38 ; bricklayer's bill (McKay & Mullison), $163 83 ; bill for lumber (Richard Price), $213,67½ ; bill for carpenter work (Peter Rementer), $276,50 ; tinman's bill (Jos. Feinour), $14,62. painter bill (Jacob Rusk), $27,37½ ; plasterer's bill (Jernan & Woodly), $57,04 ; bill for hair (Jno. Tiernan), $2,25 ; stonecutter's bill (Jno. Smith), $64,05 ; carter's bill for hauling (John Hardy), $28,94 ; sandman's bill (Jas. Quigley), $16,50 ; bills for nails (Story & McGinley), $28,31 ; bill for paints and glass (Jacob O. Wikoff), $40,21½ ; bill for bricks (C. Esling), $224,32½ ; bill for lumber, (Isaac Hozey), $10.82 ; Snyder's bill for brickwork, etc. (Snyder & Myers ; $24.58 ; Hurley's bill for paper hanging, $22.43 ; Chas. Johnson's bill, cash advanced for sundries, $73.60 ; Geo. Emlen's bill for half party wall, clergy's yard (Thomas McKay, measurer), $16,60 ; Mr Haydock's bill for introducing the water (Eden Haydock), $93.60.

Total, $1,427.08.

Deducting from the above .

Received of Rev. Mr. Rosetter for sundry jobs, $51,49 ; received of Geo. Emlen for half party wall, $40.42

Total expense	$1,335.16
John Carrell's bill of ironmongery,	26.37

$1,361.53
or £519 11s. 6d.

A £ in those days was of Pennsylvania currency. as $2.67

The itemized bills of the workmen named, and the general statement, may be examined at the American Catholic Historical Society of Philadelphia.

MARTIN I. J. GRIFFIN.

THE ATTEMPT TO ESTABLISH THE FRANCISCANS IN

PENNSYLVANIA.

In May, 1885, there came into my hands a part of a deed conveying land from Joseph Cauffman to Mark Wilcox and Rev. Mathew Carr.   The date of the paper and the location of the land could not be ascertained from the piece, but sufficient remained to show that the land was for religious purposes.

In November, 1885, while searching among the rubbish of a garret, I found papers preceding and following the piece of the deed I got in May. These papers all prove of historical value, as they relate to the attempt to establish the Franciscan Order in Pennsylvania at the beginning of this century by Rev. Michael Egan, afterwards Philadelphia's first Bishop.

The papers prove that the effort was made while he was stationed at St· Mary's Church, and not, as a well-known Catholic historical writer says, that he was appointed to that church after the failure of the attempt to establish the Order according to the authority given him by the Rescript of Sept. 29th, 1804.

Father Egan came to this country late in 1801 or early in 1802, a minister to the Catholics of Albany, N. Y. I find him in Lancaster, Pa., January 17th, 1803, the Catholics having repaid the Albany Catholics his expense from Ireland.

Father Egan came to St. Mary's, Philadelphia, April 11th, 1803. He was a Franciscan, and on September 29th, 1804, was given authority to found the Order here.

On August 6th, 1806, Joseph Cauffman conveyed to Mark Wilcox and Rev. Mathew Carr, 332¼ acres in Indiana County (late Wesmoreland County). It was called Rodesheim or Rodesham (spelled both ways in the deeds), as a site for a "house of religious worship and parsonage, and for a burial place for the use of the religious society of Roman Catholics, and for the support of a clergyman or clergymen who shall officiate there, and in confidence that they would permit the land and the buildings thereon to be erected to be under the management of the said religious society. Provided that the clergymen officiating should be of the Reverend Brethern of the Order of St. Francis, and would be appointed by the Bishop of the diocese in which the land should be." The land so conveyed by Cauffman he had obtained February 10th, 1776, from John Lesher, who had the same day obtained a warrant from it "out of the Proprietary's Land Office." [Recorded July 13th, 1776, Westmoreland County. Book A. page 131].

On Sept. 5th, 1810, Mark Willcox and Rev. Mathew Carr conveyed the land [Recorded, Indiana County, Book No. 2, page 134] to *Bishop* Egan, for the purposes and intentions declared by Cauffman in his grant to them. Bishop Egan died July 14th, 1814, intestate as regards this land. The land descended to his brother Thomas, who died intestate. His son, Rev. Michael D. Egan, on Aug. 6, 1823, conveyed the land to Bishop Conwell. [Recorded, Indiana County Deed Book No. 9, pages, 192–3–4.

There seems to have been a suit about the land in 1836. Other investigators can trace further.

This is the proof that Father Egan did secure land for the purpose of founding the Franciscan Order, and held it until his death. He may not have gone on with the work because in December, 1806, the formation of the Diocese of Philadelphia had been recommended, and it was known two years before his consecration as Bishop that he was appointed.

Joseph Cauffman was born near Strasburg, in Alsace. He died February 2d, 1807, aged eighty-eight, and is buried in St. Mary's graveyard. His son Joseph studied medicine at Vienna, and became surgeon on the United States Ship "Randolph." He was killed by an explosion on board of that vessel during the Revolution. A daughter married the Mark

Wilcox who was associated with Rev. Mathew Carr on the deed.   Nothing is known of Joseph Cauffman's first wife; but his second, the widow of Captain Butler, died Aug. 8th, 1787, aged forty-six years, and was buried in the burial ground—now Franklin Square—at the corner of Seventh and Vine.

Joseph Cauffman was intimately identified with Catholic affairs for perhaps half a century. He seems to have been closely connected with Father Harding in the purchase of properties—for the purchase would be made by Father Harding, who would immediately make declaration that it was the property of Joseph Cauffman.

Cauffman resided on Cherry street above Third on the site of the Barley Sheaf Hotel. He left a legacy to the poor widows of St. Mary's congregation. In 1769 he and John Cottringer had an Act passed in their favor by the Assembly, allowing them to hold lands in this Province, but Governor John Penn by advice of his Council refused his consent to the Bill, "as the persons named are Roman Catholics." [Colonial Records, Vol. IX.; page 596]. He is supposed to be buried at St. Mary's South Fourth street, but the grave is unknown. Yet the descendants of this gentleman are to-day Protestants. His son was an *intelligent* man and doubted transubstantiation, according to the information given me by *his* son. But a Baptist wife was no doubt the cause of the abandonment of the faith of his father. His sister, Nancy, however, was faithful, and for many years attended the adornment of St. Mary's sacristy.

Mark Wilcox was the grandfather of Mark Wilcox, at one time proprietor of the *Catholic Standard*. He was one of the incorporators of St. Mary's Church, Sept. 13th, 1788. He then was a merchant in this city. On the death of his father, Thomas Wilcox, the paper manufacturer at Ivy Mills, he succeeded to the business. He died there in 1827, aged eighty years.

Rev. Mathew Carr was the pastor of St. Augustine's Church.

The papers mentioned are now in the Manuscript Department of the American Catholic Historical Society of Philadelphia.

                                        MARTIN I. J. GRIFFIN.

FIRST CONFIRMATION IN PHILADELPHIA.

First Confirmation in Philadelphia by. Rev. John Carroll, Catholic histories and writers assign to the year 1784. After considerable search and testing statements of several writers I am satisfied that Father Carroll administered Confirmation for the first time in Philadelphia in St. Mary's Church, October 2d, 1785. Possibly the following Sunday, October 9th, may have been the day.

His appointment as Superior with power to administer this sacrament is dated June 6th, 1784. The letter of appointment came to Le Sieur Barbede Marbois, the French Vice Consul in this city, and it was not until Nov. 28th, 1784, that Dr. Carroll received it. That would have been too late in the year to have gone on a visitation from Rock Creek, Md. Besides, it would have been necessary for him to have given notice so as to have those who were to receive the sacrament properly prepared. Again no trace of Dr. Carroll's presence in Philadelphia in 1784 have I been able to discover.

But he came here in 1785, having one thing to do. That was to get the signature of aposta'e Jesuit, his cousin, Rev. C. H. Wharton, to certain papers conveying to Wharton's brother the estate in Maryland which he had surrendered before joining the Jesuits provided his brother married with the consent of Rev. Dr. Carroll. That consent having been given,

Dr. Carroll brought on necessary papers to be signed. They met for this purpose at the house of Thomas FitzSimons, where Dr. Carroll was a guest, and though they had issued controversial pamphlets against one another, they met on the most friendly terms to transact the business. [Dr. Carroll's pamphlet, in reply to Wharton's, is among the rare books in The American Catholic Historical Society of Philadelphia.] The property was in St. Mary's county, Md., but unfortunately the land records of that county for that date have been destroyed. Otherwise the date of the papers would give us the date of confirmation more nearly.

Rev. Dr. Carroll, after making visitations in Maryland, on Sept. 22d, started on "on a progress" for Philadelphia, New York and New Jersey. That date was Thursday, and perhaps he may have reached this city, by Sunday, the 25th, but considering the means of traveling in those days, and the consequent fatigue, and that Dr. Carroll is likely to have stopped at Bohemia Manor, in charge of his brethern of the then suppressed (?) Society of Jesus, and to have attended to the Catholics thereabout, it is not likely that he reached Philadelphia until during the week. The first Sunday of October (2), 1785, with a possibility of its being October 9th, may be regarded as the date of the first Confirmation in Philadelphia.

MARTIN I. J. GRIFFIN.

WASHINGTON AT MASS AND VESPERS.

In his diary, under the date of May 27th, 1787, Washington records: "Went to the Romish Church at High Mass."

He was then in Philadelphia as a delegate to the Convention to form the Constitution.

It may be objected that the words used by Washington do not prove that the church was St. Mary's, and that it might have been St. Joseph's. But there is the positive evidence of the registers that the baptisms on May 27th, 1787, were at St. Mary's, and by Father Beeston. He preached and Father Molyneux celebrated Mass.

One hundred years ago, and both less and more, St. Mary's was *the* Catholic church. There High Mass on Sundays was celebrated. Besides, there exists the plan of St. Mary's in 1787, with the names of the pew-holders. Thomas FitzSimons was a member of the Constitutional Convention, and as he was a member of St. Mary's, he, or George Meade, the grandfather of the late General George Meade, no doubt accompanied Washington, and occupied the pew of George Meade (No. 11), or that of Thomas FitzSimons (No. 12). Both were in front of the altar, or about the end of the middle aisle pews the way the church is now entered.

It was not Washington's first visit to the church. On October 9th, 1774, he made this record in his diary : "Went to the Presbyterian meeting in the morning and the Romish church in the afternoon." John Adams was with him. Here is the way Mr. Adams wrote to his wife that evening :

" This afternoon, led by curiosity and good company, I strolled away to mother Church, or rather grandmother Church—I mean the Romish chapel. I heard a good, short moral essay upon the duty of parents to their children, founded in justice and charity, to take charge of their interests, temporal and spiritual. This afternoon's entertainment was to me most awful and affecting; the poor wretches fingering their beads, chanting Latin, not a word of which they understood; their " Pater Nosters " and " Ave Marias ;" their holy water ; their crossing themselves perpetually ; their bowing to the name Jesus whenever they heard it ; their bowing and kneeling and genuflecting before the altar.

" The dress of the priest was rich with lace. His pulpit was velvet and gold. The altar-piece was rich, little images and crucifixes about, wax candles lighted up. But how shall I describe the picture of our Saviour, in a frame of marble over the altar, at full length upon the cross in the agonies, and blood dripping and streaming from His wounds ! The music, consisting of an organ and a choir of singers, went all the afternoon except sermon time, and the assembly chanted most sweetly and exquisitely. Here is everything which can lay hold of the eye, ear and imagination— everything which can charm and bewitch the simple and ignorant. I wonder how Luther ever broke the spell." [Page 45 of " Familiar Letters of John Adams to his wife Abigail, during the Revolution." By Charles Francis Adams. New York: 1876.]

MARTIN I. J. GRIFFIN.

REV. THOMAS CULLEN PIONEER IRISH

CATHOLIC PRIEST OF THE DIOCESE

OF DETROIT 1833--1862.

by Richard R Elliott

Detroit, as I have repeatedly shown in my contributions to the pages of THE AMERICAN CATHOLIC HISTORICAL RESEARCHES, is the oldest Catholic city in the Western States ; the parochial records of Ste. Anne's the mother church, now in the archives of the present church of this venerated name, are intact and continuous from February 2, 1704,—when the Martyr Recollect, Father Constantine Delhalle, recorded the baptism of Marie Therese, daughter of Antoine de la Mothe Cadillac, founder of the city—down to the present time. These records of two centuries, contain more autographs of priests than any other Catholic documentary series of manscripts in the United States ; moreover, they are well preserved, remarkably legible and solidly bound in leather according to the epochs to which they refer.

After 132 years of Catholic life—95 years of which was under Quebec, and 37 under Baltimore, Detroit became the titular city of the diocese of this historic Catholic name in American annals, in 1833.

Very Rev. Frederic Résé, Vicar General of Cincinnati, and a Roman D. D., was appointed its first Bishop.

Among the most important works inaugurated by this young and brilliant prelate, were, a seminary for the higher education of young ladies in Detroit, which he placed under the management of the Clare Sisters ; and the establishment of the College of St. Philip—Neri, in a suburb of Detroit, known at the time as Hamtramck, but which is now within the corporate limits of this city.

This college, which was intended to be the nursery of the priesthood of the new diocese, was entrusted to the care of two distinguished Oratorian Fathers from Belgium, Louis Francis Van den Poel, who was its first president, and John de Bruyn, subsequently Vicar General and joint administrator of the diocese, in conjunction with the venerable and Very Reverend Francis Vincent Badin.

St. Philip Neri was charmingly located on the high grounds of the "Church Farm," opposite Belle Isle, around which island the waters of Lake St. Clair circle, as they form the fine bay which is at the head of the straits of Detroit.

Among the faculty of this college was a young Irish gentleman, Thomas Cullen, professor of classics, who was a postulant for the priesthood. He was a native of Wexford, who had come to Cincinnati in 1832, and who became a member of the religious family of Bishop Résé, when the latter assumed possession of the See of Detroit in 1833.

Ordained priest in 1836—Father Cullen remained at the college until the death of Very Rev. Father de Bruyn in 1839; its first president Very Rev. Father Van den Poel having died in 1837.

In the meantime the first Irish Catholic parish in the Western States had been founded in Detroit; the Church of the Holy Trinity, which was dedicated on Trinity Sunday 1835. An account of this important event in American Catholic history has already been contributed by the writer to THE AMERICAN CATHOLIC HISTORICAL RESEARCHES, which includes the names, residences, and occupations, of the original congregation of this pioneer Irish Catholic Church in the Western States. Father Cullen was assigned to the pastorate of Trinity Church, by Vicar General Badin, Administrator of the diocese, in 1839. The unassuming piety, the zeal, and the warm hearted generous nature of the young priest soon won him the esteem and love of the people of Trinity parish, as well as the respect of the venerable Father Badin, and the admiration of his associates in the priesthood.

Meanwhile the parochial constituency of Trinity parish had largely increased, while the work of Father Cullen became arduous. In November 1841, Rev. Peter Paul Lefevere, missionary priest in Southern Illinois, was consecrated Bishop of Zela, and appointed administrator of the diocese of Detroit, superseding Vicar General Francis Vincent Badin, who retired to his native city Orleans, France.

Rt. Rev. Dr. Résé, the titular bishop, while enjoying the revenues of his diocese, remaining in Rome.

Among the changes which followed the advent of Bishop Lefevere, was the transfer of Father Cullen from the pastorate of Trinity Church to missionary work among the Catholic population scattered through that portion of the young State of Michigan, in the tiers of counties lying next the borders of Indiana and Ohio, and extending west from Detroit to the shores of Lake Michigan. The only parishes outside of Detroit were at Monroe and Grand Rapids.

That region of the State, rich in agricultural promise, was, at the time, being rapidly settled; not by groups and colonies of immigrant peasants from Northern Europe, as was the case in Illinois and Wisconsin, but by intelligent farmers from the older States, having means to cultivate the soil, and by fairly well to do Irish and English agriculturists, who bought quarter sections of fine land at government prices and made new homes for themselves and families. In the new population, and especially among the Irish immigrants, was a considerable percentage of people who had been reared in the Catholic faith.

A glance at the map of the Lower Peninsula of Michigan, will enable the reader to form an estimate of the extent of that part of Michigan then being settled, by taking the northerly line of the counties of Oakland, Livingston, Ingham, Eaton, Barry and Allegan, including these and Washtenaw, Jackson, Calhoun, Kalamazoo, Van Buren, Lenawe, Hillsdale, Branch St Joseph, Cass, and Berrien; to all these should be added Shiawassee just north of Ingham and Livingston counties.

This extensive territory was bounded by Indiana and Ohio and on the west by Lake Michigan.

The State of Michigan had in progress of construction, a railroad from Detroit to Chicago; extending from the former city through the counties of Wayne, Washtenaw, Jackson, Calhoun, Kalamazoo, Van Buren, and Berrien, directly west and around the southern shore of Lake Michigan to the future metropolis of the Western States. At the time of Father Cullen's transfer from Detroit, the Michigan Central Railroad, as it has since been called, had been completed to Ann Arbor in Washtenaw County, and this city became the headquarters of Father Cullen's missionary operations. A daily train was operated between Detroit and Ann Arbor, while as this city was 40 miles from the metropolis of the State, its railroad terminal facilities made it an important factor in the receipt of agricultural products, and in the distribution of food and merchandize from Detroit to the interior counties. It was at Ann Arbor, that passengers destined for the west, after a ride of 40 miles on a *flat rail*, entered the stage coaches and open wagons, to continue their journeys along the " mail routes," many of which had been but recently developed.

Ann Arbor at the time of Father Cullen's advent, was a busy place ; and of far more commercial importance than the city is at the present day.

It was fortunate for Father Cullen that he had been blessed with more than ordinary physical proportions ; he was over 6 feet, and at the time, not far from 200 pounds weight His face was of true Milesian outline, his large eyes blue ; and his hair light auburn. Such was the exterior man.

But the heart that beat within that stalwart frame was angelic ; Father Cullen entwined his affection around the nature of those he loved with such indissoluble bonds as to be sundered only with the end of life.

I knew him first in the class room where commenced a friendship which never ceased during his life. This friendship at an early day ripened into intimacy, which continued during his priestly career ; I have witnessed his triumphs in the missionary field, and it was my privilege to cheer and console him when heavy crosses and trials so moved and grieved his great and generous heart, that he wept almost in despair. It is a great satisfaction to write in praise of a dear friend—even if in so doing memories are evoked which had their beginning long before the present generation were born.

Warm as these memories are, they shall not cause my pen to deviate from historic verity in the outline which I shall attempt to trace of Father Cullen's missionary career ; but I will say his work was apostolic during its continuance, and it was probably known and best appreciated by the Divine Master he served. It was moreover destined to be without parallel in the missionary annals of Michigan, except in the glorious record of Father Richard ; and in the evangelical labors and physical privations of the saintly Bishop Baraga, among the unfortunate Indian tribes of the Upper Peninsula.

That fair portion of the Lower Peninsula of Michigan now covered with cities and towns and traversed in all directions by railways and good roads, was, during the earlier years of Father Cullen's missionary labors, only partly redeemed from its primitive wildness, by the sparse settlements of the enterprising pioneers whose own and whose children's labor has since transformed the solitude of the forest to the fairest agricultural region, probably to be found in the Western States.

The roads throughout the extensive circuit of his mission, which extended from the Huron River to the shore of Lake Michigan, during the greater part of the year were so bad, that the journeys which had to be made in the saddle and on foot would have been impossible for the average man ; they were accomplished, however, and the consolations of religion brought to the scattered families by the priestly visits of Father Cullen, whose administration of the Sacraments of the Church and whose wise and sincere exhortations were no doubt the means of perpetuating the Catholic faith in the hearts of many and in bringing others into the fold. It was thus he laid the foundation of the extensive Catholic population existing in this important section of Michigan at the present day.

While this missionary work was in its inception, the political status of the government of Michigan had been completely changed. The party succeeding to power decided to abandon the work of building railroads which it must be admitted, had not been a success.

The Michigan Central Railroad was sold to a syndicate of Boston capitalists, to whom a liberal and perpetual charter was granted, on condition that the road be completed as rapidly as possible through the State to Chicago. Under the same title was formed the company which completed this work.

Its president was John W. Brooks who came to Detroit to build this road.

He was a man endowed with all the requisites necessary, with millions of capital at his command. His staff included Colonel John M. Berrien, a West Point topographical engineer, and Reuben N. Rice, a relative of the President, disbursing officer in the construction of the roadway and for the right of way.

The names of Colonel Berrien and Mr. Rice, are mentioned, because with these two estimable gentlemen, Father Cullen became intimately associated in beneficent work in behalf many inexperienced Irish laborers employed during the construction of the roadway, whose line Westward soon became covered with the shanties of Irish Catholic laborers and their families. The advent of this element increased the missionary duties of Father Cullen. Fortunate indeed was it, that these strangers had the advice and spiritual assistance of such a saintly man as was Father Cullen. He was a disciple of Father Matthew, while no mercenary thought ever had a place in his generous heart. Though the co operation of Colonel Berrien and of Mr. Rice, very many of the laborers purchased government land and thus acquiring homes, became citizens and the founders of Catholic families. By the advice of the missionary, others of the same class, sent money to provide means for the passage to Michigan of their families in Ireland and thus new homes were formed in the towns and cities between Ann Arbor and Kalamazoo.

In the developement of his missionary work Father Cullen made Jackson, Marshall, and Kalamazoo, centres, which he connected with subordinate tributary stations, which he visited at stated times regularly.

By this wise division of his work, he was enabled to establish a chain of parishes extending along the line of the Michigan Central Rail Road from Ann Arbor to Niles, and to promote the building of churches in the cities named.

When pastors were subsequently appointed to these churches, they took up the work inaugurated by Father Cullen and made regular visits to the tributary stations of each parochial centre. In this manner, by the heroic efforts and by the saintly labors of Father Cullen, as stated, was the foundation laid, a half century ago, of the extensive Catholic population residing in the tiers of counties I have named, which formed the theatre of his missionary circuits. But, when one after another, priests took up their residences in the city parishes, and assumed the spiritual care of the faithful in the subordinate stations, until finally the counties west of Washtenaw were all provided with spiritual care, the missionary work of Father Cullen was practically accomplished.

It was a great work, and it was well done; while it has been perpetuated by many zealous and holy priests.

While Ann Arbor had always been the missionary home of Father Cullen, he was necessarily absent for months during certain seasons of the year; this city now became his permanent residence.

He had in the meantime built and partly completed a fine church, which he had dedicated in honor of his patron, St. Thomas. Selecting a location on a hill side overlooking the city and surrounding territory, he purchased an acre of land on which he built an agreeable rural home, which he surrounded with ornamental grounds laid out in good taste. He had contributed much of his private means to the building of the Church of St. Thomas, and for its completion, and what he was lacking for the completion of his home was cheerfully contributed by friends in Ann Arbor and Detroit. In the meantime one of the brothers of Father Cullen, who had been a merchant in Wexford, had died, leaving a widow and two children, a boy and girl, with but moderate means for their support. He sent funds to provide for the passage of his brother's widow and children and on their arrival at Ann Arbor, Mrs. Cullen was placed in charge of his rural home. She was an educated, intelligent lady, of amiable disposition, and while she made the priest's household agreeable she made herself useful as his secretary in parochial work.

Many Irish and some German farmers had settled in the vicinity of Ann Arbor, and in the townships of Washtenaw County.

The spiritual interest of these families had constant attention ; to visit them, did not require the toilsome journeys of former days ; the county had been will developed, the roads were good, the country rolling, and it became an agreeable exercise for Father Cullen to drive in his light carriage through one of the most beautiful regions in the State, when making these periodical visitations, or when he was called to perform sacerdotal offices to the sick.

But Ann Arbor had become greatly changed.

After the city had ceased to be the terminal of the Michigan Central, its commercial importance ceased. The University of Michigan which had been most liberally endowed by the State, had been gradually progressing on the road to eminence, and was already a flourishing institution, with increasing numbers of students at each commencement.

Among its faculty were several eminent scholars and scientists. Ann Arbor had become a university city, but it was also the home of some of the ablest lawyers and shrewdest politicians in the State.

Although the president and faculty of the University were unanimously non-Catholic, the position Father Cullen occupied, and that Free Masonry of intellect which unites all sects in scholarly fellowship among educated men, made the Catholic priest the esteemed and respected associate of the learned, in the collegiate and professional circles of Ann Arbor.

With such surroundings ; with a sympathetic constituency and living in his home made agreeable by a refined lady, Father Cullen spent the last and most agreeable decade of his sacredotal existence.

He greatly enjoyed the society of his intimate friends.

When I could snatch a few days of, leisure from the exactions of
business, I would say to my wife, "pack our grips and let us go to Father
Cullen and enjoy ourselves." He was very abstemious, used no wine at
his table, nor did he smoke, but he had a capacious snuff box ; and yet, it
gave him pleasure to see his visitors smoke the fragrant cigars he was
always happy to offer them. He was childishly fond of a game of cards and
followed its chances with intense interest.

He was witty and could appreciate the humorous in ordinary events,
while his excellent memory enabled him to detail many ludicrous events
which had come under his obervation.

One of these is worth a place in this outline of his career.

The administrator of the diocese, Bishop Lefevere, had recruited his
priesthood with young seminarians from Belgium and Holland ; good young
men, as a rule, but unused, either to the English language, or to the
manners and customs of English speaking communities. The vicar general of the diocese and theological instructor of the ecclesiastical students,
and a fellow countryman of the bishop, was Very Rev. Peter Kindekens, a
most exemplary priest but little used to American life or manners.

Mrs. Cullen had for assistant and general housework an Irish dame of
mature years and of no very amiable disposition ; while she respected the
house keeper, she worshipped the priest and heeded his behests, one of
which was to admit no one during the absence of himself and of her
mistress.

It happened one October afternoon while the housekeeper was on a
visit to Detroit, that Father Cullen had gone on a missionary visit to a
neighboring village and was to return at 6 o'clock.

Meanwhile the ancient dame was in charge.

About 3 o'clock a dignified appearing gentleman in priestly attire and
carrying a grip entered the pastoral gate and rung the door bell. The dame
partly opened the door, and as the vicar was about to push his way in she
prevented him and asked his business. "I want to see *Mr.* Cullen " he
replied. " *Father* Cullen is away on the mission and will be home at 6
o'clock," the dame responded and was about to close the door. "But I
must come in," said the vicar who was now slightly ruffled.

"My orders are to admit nobody while the priest is away." "But I
must come in my good woman," insisted the vicar.

" You can't come into this house I tell you," said the angry dame.

The vicar replied with dignity, " I must come in for I am the Vicar General."

The dame with a resolute look replied, "I don't care if you were " Gineral " Jackson himself, I would not let you in," and closed and bolted the door.

When about 6 o'clock Father Cullen drove home and entered his grounds, he found the Vicar pacing the gravel walk and reading his office ; he was greatly irritated, and as he related his experience, with the final emphatic allusion to " Gineral " Jackson, the good natured missionary had much difficulty in restraining his mirth ; while the Vicar General of Detroit and " Gineral " Jackson, for some years caused many a laugh when the story was related to his intimate friends.

Father Cullen was a man who was true to his God, to his Country, and to the memory of his Fatherland.

All three in their order he loved and served : His God in the priesthood, his country as a patriotic American citizen, and his native land as a generous true hearted Irishman.

His hard work while on the missionary circuit ; his days in the saddle ; his nights without sleep and his uncertain and at times indifferent food and lodging, made no apparent effect on his robust and splendid physique, while all these exaction upon his system were being endured. But it is probably impossible, to abuse the admirable and finely constructed mechanism of the human body in any of its parts, from the bottom of the foot to the scalp of the head, without each of such injuries being placed to account against the general welfare of the organization, to be paid for in time, by some fatal affiction of some one organ, which may be essential to the harmonious functions of the human system.

Strongly constructed as he was, he had to pay the penalty of overwork and incessant fatigue in the organic malady which terminated fatally September 7th, 1862, when he was called to his eternal reward in the 58th year of his age.

The poor and the distinguished followed the remains of the dead missionary to the tomb prepared in the church of his patron saint. No such demonstration had ever been seen, or has since been witnessed in the streets of Ann Arbor, as was on that day. A third of a century has passed since this event, How agreeable it is to me to recall the memories connected with such a saintly man and such a sincere friend ; and how grateful the task to place an outline of his career on the imperishable tablets of the history of the Catholic Church in America.

RICHARD R. ELLIOTT.

Detroit July 1896.

OLD ST. MARY'S, PHILADELPHIA, CONTRIBUTORS TO

THE ALTERATION AND IMPROVEMENT OF THE

CHURCH IN 1809--10--11.

THE FOLLOWING SUBSCRIPTIONS WERE RECEIVED IN RESPONSE

TO THE APPEAL TO ENLARGE ST. MARY'S CHURCH.

PHILADELPHIA,

June 24th, 1809.

Geo. Nugent,	$100	Matthew Lyons,	$10
Keran Fitzgerald,	10	Jno. Donaher,	20
Patrick Gernan,	20	Jno. Leamy,	10
July 14, Paul Bustee,	100	Aug. 2, Mrs. Montgomery,	100
Oct. 5, Terance Bryne,	20	Oct. 6, Cap. Jno. Rossiter,	500

1810.

Jan. 29, John Ashley,	1,000	R. Brown,	5
Feb. 2, Jas. Eneu,	100	Berd'. Connor,	10
Mar. 28, Neil Boyle,	40	D. Edwin,	10
Greg. Straban,	5	Wm. Keating,	5
Jacob Holaban,	16	Chas. Hagarty,	5
Jno. Hickey,	5	Morgan Carr,	100
Patrick Delany,	10	Hugh Turney,	5
Nicholas Lambert,	5	Jno. Byrne,	10
Jno. Smith,	25	Jno. Hart,	5
Thos. Hickey,	10	Joseph Marble,	10
Harper & McGuire,	10	Dan'l. Kane,	5
Cornelius Haveland,	3	Patrick Mallon,	10
Victor Haudue,	2	Wm. Hanagan,	1
Jno. Mount,	5	Jno. Fife,	5

Apr. 12. Jasper Moylan,	200	J. C. Sarmeinto,	150
Edw. Barry,	150	Chas. C. Springer,	150
Cath. Mallon,	100	Thos. Peacan,	20
Lewis Clapier,	300	Tos. Newman,	150
Capt. John Meaney,	150	Jno. Savage,	150
Jos. Dugan,	150	Jno. Keating,	100
Lewis Ryan,	200	Augusn Bousquet	100
Thos. W. Francis	50	Thos. M. Willing,	50
A. & J. Walker, & Co.	50	French Consoul,	10
Berd'. Gallagher,	100	Mich. Williamson,	3
Wm. Whelan,	20	Jas. Brady,	10
Jno. McDermott,	10	Jos. Synder,	150
Jno. Gilson,	50	Capt. M. D. Dougherty	100
Patrick Carlan,	10	James Gibson,	50
Capt. P. O'Brion,	50	Eliza Collins,	10
Jno. B. Guenet,	10	Felix McQuaid,	15
Jno. McGuigan,	50	Philip Smith,	200
Mrs. —— Risdel,	50	Francis Lynch,	20
Wm. Boyle,	5	Anthony Groves,	100
Jno. T. Sullivan,	25	W. Leary,	10
Jno. Gartland,	5	Thos. Reily,	10
Jas. Toner,	20	Peter Lambert,	10
Michael Doweas,	10	Matthew Flood,	5
Mich. Durney,	100		

June 7, Robert Mercer,	5	Dan'l. McGill,	5
Jos. Carroll,	10	Jas McCafferty,	20
Mich. Foy,	4	Jno. Bristland.	5
John Dempsey,	5	Mrs. Linnerd,	3
Isaac Lott,	10	Dennis Christy,	5
Jas. Maguire,	5	Laurence O'Brien,	5
Anthony Plumb,	2	Ann Kallala,	10
Arthur McGinniss,	10	Ann Caufman,	40
Chas. Taws,	100	E· J. Guien and Bion,	50
Bishop Egan for unknown person		$2.50.	
Anthony Steel,	100	Mich. Neal,	20
Capt. Patrick Hays,	100	Hugh Cavanaugh,	100
Patrick Boyle,	1	Jas. Garvey,	1
Jno. Guyet,	1.50	Mich. Heasey,	2

June 8. Patrick Brutin,	5	Patrick Martin,	10
Michael Roark,	5	Arthur Means,	5
Patrick Bradley,	5	Patrick McKeevan,	5
Patrick Brady,	5	Michael Size,	5
Martin Kennedy,	5	Michael Fortune,	50

June 19 Nicholas Lafevre,	20	27	Charles Smith,	50
21, Margaret Caufman,	50	28	John Bohlen,	50
25 Bernard Sleman,	1		Thomas Hurley, Jun.	25
Maria C. Hammond,	10	29	Jeremiah Sullivan,	10.37
Patrick Malloy,	10	30	James Henderson, Esqr.	20
John Riely,	5			

July 2	Francis Harrison,	5	July 10 Francis Doyle,	8
	Mary Black,	5	13 Bernard Conway,	20
	Barney McCabe,	5	Michael Kane,	10
	James Tawes,	1	John Deane,	2
	James Boyle,	5	John McCormick,	5
	Redmond Byrne for Gerard Byrne,			200
	Terance McNulty,	5	14 Henry O'Neill,	50
	Thomas Mooney,	3	Geffey Purtell,	10
3	Thomas McEune,	50	Sarah Egan	3
6	Cornelius Tears,	30	17 Mich. McGrath,	120
	Peter Inemez,	3	19 Edward Cassidy,	10
	John Denver,	5	23 Daniel Williamson,	1
	Patrick Hughes,	5	Michael McGill,	5
	John Dolan,	5	Mrs. Leib,	20
	Peter Farley,	10	John Leahey,	5
	John Barry,	5	John Byrne,	40
8	Thomas Grady,	5	H. Duffy,	5
	Felix Meguigan.	5	Cornelius McBride,	1.50
	Philip Brady,	.75	George McKinney,	1
	Francis Keran,	5	John McGee,	4
	Anthony Campbell,	10	John McDevitt,	5
9	James McHill,	20	29 Francis Duffy,	5
9	John Doyle, Pd. $100, & Aug. 17th, Pd. $100	200		
	Eleanor Green,	10	George Allen,	5
	Jos. Gallagher,	10	F. Morgan,	5
10	James McGill,	20	John McBride,	1.50
	Eleanor Green,	10	30 John Melanefy,	2

Aug. 6.	Berd. Connor,	10	Aug. 16	John Reilly,	10
	Robt. Harwood,	50	20	Jeremiah Nicholas,	15
	M. McClaskey,	5		Neil McGinley,	3
	Charles O'Hara,	5		Thos. Hickey,	10
11	Thos. Maher,	15	21	Patrick Hogan,	75
	Cornelius McManus,	5	23	Harper McGuire,	10
12	Edw. Mullan,	50	26	Peter Harkins,	10
13	Stephen Girard,	100		Peter Scravendyke,	100
14	Hugh Christy,	100		Neil Fearon,	20
	Daniel Flaherty,	5		John Garvin,	5
	Law Caufman,	50		Bernard Daily,	5
16	Cornelius O'Donnell,	10		Wm. McCormick,	5
	Darby McCurran,	5	27	John Maitland,	100
	John Hart,	5		Mathew Carey,	50
	Law Handy,	10		John Angue,	25
	James McGinley, In hauling Sand,				20

Sept. 2	Edw. John McVey,	25	Sept. 9.	James Haveland,	5
	Thomas McLean,	50		Peter Provencheir,	20
	Michael Cooper,	2		John Doyle, Market St.	10
	Charles McCabe,	5	9	Thomas Ash,	15
	James Harvey,	5		Neil Hawkins,	2
	Bernard O'Donnell,	10		Felix Campbell,	5
	Vincent DuCamb,	100		Bartholomy Kelly,	5
	Peter Poland or Palin,	20		Daniel Queen,	10
	Michael Hickey,	10		James Nickham,	5
4	Joseph Danolth,	100		Nicholas Moloy,	3
	Eleanor Kelly,	50		Daniel O'Brion,	10
5	Captain Francis Wm. V. Reyngan,				200
8	Lewis Roberts,	1	26	John Connelly,	50
	Morris Collins,	5		John O'Brien,	10
	Anthony Gallagher,	5	27	John Dubarry.	100

Oct. 1 Charles Caney,	20	Nov. 13 Christopher Brady,	2
Joseph Fernen,	10	Charles Johnson,	200
Sarah Elizabeth Ashley,	40	20 John Breschard,	150
Thomas Burk,	5	Victor Pepine,	150
Timothy Haran,	3	22 Francis Breuil,	100
Rachael Myers,	150	M. McDermott,	10
Charles Calaughan,	15	John Boyle, in Sand,	111
8th Lewis Roberts,	10	John Burke,	5
Richard Williams,	10	Mrs. Lieb,	30
11 Edward McDermott,	100	Manasses O'Donnell,	5
15 John Kelly,	10	John McMullon,	5
Joseph Marble,	10	J. C. Sarmlente,	100
17 Anthony Huniker,	25	Mrs. Lieb,	10
18 Patrick Callan,	100	Nicholas Lambert	50
22 John Herky,	15	John Griffith,	100
23 Louis D. Carpenter,	5	Abraham Pruene,	10
24 Andrew McGee,	1	Patrick M. McCafferty,	20
Bartholomy Larozin,	150	Bridget O'Donnell,	5
28 Edward Mullin,	50	Danile Guerey,	50
Daniel Gourley,	50	John Latair,	20
Nov. 2. Henry Harberger,	20	T. L. Ketland for R. Ketland,	550
Wm. McElroy,	5	Michael Lambert,	50
11 Thomas McClean,	50	Thomas Fitzsimons,	100
14 Anthony Graves,	110	Jos. A. Wigmore,	5
Hugh Christy,	50		
Henry O'Neill,	60	Nicholas Esling,	150
Christopher O'Connor,	25	Mrs. Leib,	20
Wm. Calliebaus,	10	Isaac Hazey,	200
18 Charles Hagerty,	5		

1811, January 2nd.

Amos Holahan,	110	Michael Durney,	50
John Burke,	5	James Eneu,	35
B. Sarozau,	50	Ann Cauffmann,	10
Berd. Gallagher,	30	George Nugent,	100
Wm. Keating,	5	Dan'l. Dougherty,	60.75
Joseph Charles Springer,	100	D. McArthur,	10
Don Lewis De Onis, Spanish Minister,			600
Peter McScully,	28	Lewis Ryan,	75
James Boyle,	50	John Keating,	20
Timothy Currin,	175	Captain John Meaney,	50
Jasper Moylan, Esq.	25	Thomas Hurley, Sr.	50
Nicholas Esling,	25	Capt. Chris O'Conner,	50
Augustine Bousquet,	60	Thomas Tompkins,	50
Fras. Mongon,	15	Fras. Higgins,	100
Jno. Saulner,	5	Jno. Byrne,	50
Wm. Smith,	20	Wm. Alingham,	20
Thos. Reilly,	25	Mrs. Lieb,	10
Henry O'Neill,	50	Mich. Roark,	10
Mich. Waltman,	120	Thos. Hickey,	50
Jno. Doyle,	50	Felix McGuigan,	5
Jas. Brady,	50	Mrs. Leib,	10
B. Mahony,	5	Chas. Johnson,	25
M. McFadden,	5	D. Connor,	5
A. Graves,	15	H. O'Neill,	100
Capt. C. O'Conner,	25	Jos. Dinath,	50
Capt. Martin Dougherty,	50	Haydeck & Stewart,	18
L. Dougherty,	5	John Bardin,	5
Jos. Rush,	8.50	James Mooney,	10
P. Callan,	5	H. Gavanagh,	50
Harper McGuire,	20	Mich. Callaghan,	11
Jas. Haviland,	20	Adam Eckfelt,	10
Geo. A. Wray,	50	Patk. Cunningham,	17.70
Jno. Smith,	75	John Maitland,	35
Patk. Devitt,	10	Jas. Quigley,	37
Peter Dalamer,	50	Peter McGuiley,	30
Henry O'Neill,	150	Capt. G. Byrne.	100
Tim Desmond,	125	Phillip McCormack,	5
Anth Steel,	66	Mr. Gardette,	100
Dan'l. Dougherty,	59.25	Peter Laysang,	10
Jno. Rea,	16.55	Jas. M. Byrne,	25
Chas. Tawes,	50	Geo. Magragh,	50
Rich. Myers,	60	Jno. T. Sullivan,	25
Anth Renento,	5	V. DuCumb,	50
Morgan Carr,	30	Jos. Synder,	60
Edw. John McVey,	10	Jos. Rush,	8.50

Total, $16,721.42

The

AMERICAN ✻ CATHOLIC

Historical Researches.

VOLUME XIII, 1896.

The first law of History is not to dare tell a lie; the second not to fear to tell the truth; besides let the Historian be beyond all suspicion of favoring or hating anyone whomsoever. LEO XIII.

Which if I have done well and as becometh the history is what I have desired; but if not so perfectly it must be pardoned me. MACHABEES XV, 39.

✻ PUBLISHED ✻ AND ✻ EDITED ✻

BY

MARTIN I. J. GRIFFIN,

No. 711 SANSOM STREET,

PHILADELPHIA.

CONTENTS, 1896.

www.ingramcontent.com/pod-product-compliance
Lightning Source LLC
Chambersburg PA
CBHW022042080426
42733CB00007B/949